Wi

A collection of autoethnographic poems.

Poems by
E.D. Woodford

Edited by
Deb Martens

© 2017, E.D. Woodford

All rights reserved. No part of this book may be reproduced for any reason, by any means, without the permission of the publisher.

Cover design by Consciously Inspired Press and Darcie Wright of West Coast Creative Girl

Woodford, E.D., author
        Wild Heart. Gypsy Soul. / E.D. Woodford.

Poems.
ISBN 9781973383697

Consciously Inspired Press
consciouslyinspired@gmail.com

Deb Martens, Editor
debsmartens@gmail.com

--- To the strong women in my life who listen without judgement and always provide support, kindness and opportunities for laughter. ---

Table of Contents

wild heart	9
entrust	10
the imperfect gift of love	11
you belong	12
Who are you meant to be?	13
falling in love with life	14
unbreakable love	15
beautiful uncertainty	16
under the moonlight	18
Sexy	19
first date	20
tears	21
live with wild authenticity	22
broken heels	23
on childhood crushes	24
September Sunday	27
a huckleberry romance	28
finding your happy place	29
Sunday goals	30
dancing around the bush	31
fate	32

Am I willing to reclaim time to think?	33
	33
What are you scared of?	34
kiss a lot of frogs	37
awakening	38
when I knew	39
4 Days	40
cowboy love	41
expect	42
new love	43
19 / 41	44
telling you	45
soulmate	46
chasing silence	47
a redneck love story	48
life goes on	49
wildfires	50
soul joy	51
love regardless of colour	52
on second chances	54
gypsy soul	55
Acknowledgements	56
About the Author	57

wild heart

Are you brave enough
to love me
wholeheartedly
unconditionally
with the courage
to savour my
wild heart?

entrust

entrust your wild heart to
the lover who cherishes your
messy beauty
beholds charm in your free spirit
and gypsy soul
shares unpredictable kisses
enduring kindness
and vulnerability to express
serendipitous truth and
essences of their own heart

the imperfect gift of love

the imperfect gift of love
    between friends
are cherished memories
    deep kisses
spontaneous adventures
    spring camping on a blanket of snow
lost virginity
    and dreams of tomorrow

you belong

you belong among wildflowers
rising to the morning light
a whisper as your soul's blossom awakens

you belong among wildflowers
each brave petal unique
dancing a dance of authenticity in the meadow of imperfection

you belong among wildflowers
feeling free to write
wild seeds blooming your creativity

Who are you meant to be?

without masks disguising
your past desires
your present wishes
without expectation to live without joy
without hesitation to be discovered
and without judgement
be honest

Who are you meant to be?

listen to your soul
your heart
your core being
inviting joy
inviting dreams
create your true self with
authenticity

Who are you meant to be?

falling in love with life

watching the northern lights
holding hands on the snow covered arctic.

showering in a secluded waterfall
our feet standing in the swirling pool of Copper Falls.

creating art en plein air canvas
two sets of hands intuitively painting on the river's edge.

a moonlight kayak under glittering stars
followed by the midnight skinny dip in the freshwater lake.

unbreakable love

let's place a love lock
inscribed with our initials
on the tattered park fence
and throw away
the key
of unbreakable love

beautiful uncertainty

the moment I met him Rosenheim
recalling the connection
our inquisitiveness about one another
surprising our mutual friends
unarranged
a lightening fascination
with beautiful uncertainty

English, French, German, Austrian
dinner at his parents' townhouse
a multilingual affair
amongst the three of them
incomprehensible words
of German
he succumbed to a language of mine
and our world became small and unpretentious
as we made do

in his loft
he introduced me to artistic life
music, painting and industrial installation
glimpses of dreamery
and visions
for a creative life of my own

we ran away together
to the magnificent cloud-shredding Alps

and small, quaint towns of Bavaria
nonetheless
arrived a final day in Vienna
discovering
Mozart, Beethoven, the Opera
and the medieval Catholic Cathedral
filled with cherubic heads and frescoes

that final night,
he described our medieval marriage
I as his regent Queen
solemn promises and 40 days
a blue dress of purity
an orange blossom crown
spiced wine and a feast.

I contemplated his proposal
while savouring bavarian gelato,
each other and the beautiful uncertainty.

under the moonlight

Your hands
entwined around mine pulling each other closer
Your eyes
confident, compassionate, reaching my heart
Your lips
silencing my questions, engaging my curiosity
Your name
whispering permission to my desires
under the moonlight

Sexy

You know what is sexy?
Intelligence
Kindness
Conversation
Courage
Truth
Faith
Love

first date

How redneck is the girl
whose idea of a perfect first date
is an adventure along the Moyie River Road
meandering around Sinclair Lake
 following Meadow Creek
ending with bbq and cowboy action shooting
shiny pistols
and the scent of sweet charcoal smoke?

tears

June conversations on a hot day
long distance confessions
jolting secrets
truth and revelation provokes
a rolling surge of tears
dismay, fear, and sadness

Yet, under a dark summer sky
glittering stars reflect
tears of pleasure and joy
for the present and
wishes for the future

live with wild authenticity

expect nothing

wander without destination

tame uncontrolled longing

by loving as if this will be your last love.

be vulnerable

embrace yourself

live with wild authenticity

broken heels

chronicles of mid-life crisis
at first I hope for a rescue
changing my mind
the wisdom of failure
this must be the place
a bend in the road
life is sweet
one day at a time
enduring courage
dancing through life
in a pair of broken heels

on childhood crushes

young love
the magic of childhood crushes
and the first kiss

an old vintage postcard
a young girl in a red dress
white bonnet hiding her face
the blush of shyness
a boy in blue jean overalls leans in
to steal a kiss
embracing her shoulders to steady her

an older boy next door
bothersome and meddlesome
ran and biked about the neighborhood
with an arrogance of ownership
two years older
two years more adventurous

I had a crush on him.

during a game of hide and seek
he found me
my face was blushed
with youthful shyness
but I was eager to experience the kiss
an age when

relationship possibilities were
created at recess and
dissolved by lunchtime
giggles resplendent of the innocence
of simple childhood experiences
and first crushes

twenty five years later
I check my online messages
a chat pop-up springs onto the screen
"go to bed"
a message from that first crush.
chatting ensues deep into the night
and finally, his invitation arrives
 "while you are in town next week
we should go for coffee."

the following weeks
more chatting and at some point
he declares
he is looking forward to
kissing me again
I groaned
coffee becomes more than coffee
as the sun rises
words become riskier
and chats do not cease until the
morning magenta rises in sky
above our sleepless nights.

I had a crush on him.

he doesn't know
I saw him months before
in Walmart as his girlfriend
arrived pulling him down an aisle.
"He looked hot!"
I told my friends
c'est la vie
I never would
have had the courage
to ask him out

the moment arrived.
another kiss
with my first crush.
with a naturalness that forgets
the quarter century since the first kiss
sparks a continuance
a short silence
we pulled apart before
I giggled
"Why are you laughing?"
"because this kiss was definitely better
than our first kiss."

September Sunday

I wish every Sunday could be
that one September Sunday
waking to the brisk morning air
the sounds of children's hushed voices
our tender kisses whisper faith filled wishes
and the simplicity of spending time together
joyful moments and peaceful prayers

a huckleberry romance

baby sleeping in a sling across my breasts
his revolver in my half full berry basket
the vast valley surrounding us
he knelt
on bended knee beneath
the backcountry huckleberry bramble
along the rocky incline
on the mountainous slope of Copper Ridge
and yearningly asked
"Will you marry me?"

finding your happy place

on the land
in the mountains
without destination
beyond purpose and haste
roaming through lanky pine trees
veiling the day's light
rustling needles and cones with
gratifying footsteps
along the subtle path
colours flourishing of
rejuvenation. serenity. stillness. solitude.
letting the mind rest of
unwavering thoughts.
cherished moments and
hesitations
revealing sunshine and truth
transcendent glimpses of clarity

Sunday goals

write poetry
drink good coffee
enjoy the fire
kiss a redneck on the porch
chase spontaneous adventures

dancing around the bush

living life with re-connections
laughter that awakens the soul
sunshine and firewood
rifles leaning in the cab
of a dusty pickup
camouflage clothing
dancing around the bush
with timid flirtation

fate

recently someone asked,
"What do you want?"
I paused
    What do I want?
I want to be happy
and I want to control my fate

Am I willing to reclaim time to think?

time to think

time to notice

time to slow down

time to appreciate

what is truly important with

clarity

courage

intention

and purpose

What are you scared of?

at the port of Trois-Rivieres
waiting in the 21 degree weather
the wind came off the river and
waves crashed to cemented sides
I leaned over the the rails
waiting for the arrival

empty of vessels
100 people milled around waiting
waiting for the Navy
to arrive and dock.
twenty minutes
the ship came into sight
an enormous majestic vision
on the river arriving
under the route 55 bridge
a slow entrance to the francophone port

without ceremony
we were invited aboard the ship
touring
from cabin steering to dining room
in the mechanical room
I heard someone approaching
face-to-face
with the most beautiful black man
that I had ever seen in
his white Navy uniform

he truth is

I had never really seen black men
before Quebec
and in Quebec
they were everywhere
and in Quebec
I discovered their allure.

we both stood there
looking at each other
he finally asked
"You speak English?"
time stood still a little longer
before I was able to answer
 "Yes, I speak English."
"Why don't you have an accent?"
he asked in his heavily French accented English
"Because I come from British Columbia?"
I found myself with few words
a moment of rarity

painful small talk
introductions
a personal tour of the ship
intriguing glances from his fellow sailors
as he described every facet
of the navy vessel
in the helm
my photo taken at the ship's wheel
amongst the crowd
an hour with this beautiful black man
felt like minutes that I never wanted to end

silence
as we run into my friends
we stared at each other
locked gaze destined for eternity
he grabbed my hand
and pulled me towards
his navy white uniformed body
lightly pressing me
against the side of the ship

"Meet me tonight"
he said urgently
I hesitated
tongue-tied
the answer was in my head
yet soundless
in the French language.
"What are you scared of?"
he whispered

"Everything"

kiss a lot of frogs

how do you know who is THE ONE
when the guy turned out not to be
through sickness and in health
even before the wedding day?

a gal can get a reputation after 8 proposals.
progressive. independent. modern.
but let's face it
these are not the descriptions that men use

the truth is
there's a lot of commitment to be had
from a wild heart that only knows love and kindness
yet never experiences sweet reciprocation

you have to kiss a lot of frogs.

awakening

radiance of morning light
emerging gently
illuminating
mountainous shadows
honey glow of sunrise
glistening glow off tranquil water
rejuvenated. energized.
ready to take on the world
consciously
quietly
with intention and purpose
curiosity and passion
reclaiming time

when I knew

suddenly life is a moment in slow motion
can I run away?
> *can't think*
> *curling up tight*

trapped in thoughts about him
out of sync
warm and tingly
endless smiling and passion to share love
feeling strong
> *yet fragile*

flawed
> *yet accepted*

when I knew
love is like a panic attack
fireworks exploding continuously in my heart

4 Days

let us share 4 days
shorn of limitations
to heal our unforgotten broken hearts
resolve our troubled past
and create evocative memories
of sweet naked mornings
in entwined breathlessness
of lazy afternoons
along the rocky river's edge
of gentle evenings
under the darkness of the new moon
without apprehension of the future

cowboy love

idle windmills
barbed wiring fencing
hefty round hay bales
red barns
steel silos
golden fields
boots off and hats strewn
cowboy love
under a dusty sunset

expect

I don't expect you to understand
that I must be a strong woman

I don't expect you to understand
that I must survive the struggle

I don't expect you to understand
that I must live with passion

I don't expect you to understand
that I must have you on my adventure

new love

Have you ever seen
anything in your life
more wonderful
than wandering through a field
of wildflowers holding hands
grass brushing
against bare legs
laughter amongst
the breezing wind
magnifying the discovery and
the radiance of new love
in life's joyful journey?

19 / 41

Nineteen

I didn't ask you to stay

but I didn't ask you to go either

Forty-One

I won't ask you to stay

but I won't ask you to go either

telling you

at this moment
amidst the mountain's splendour
of blooming wildflowers
and snow capped peaks
along the river's edge
I am confident telling you
what I will tell no one

soulmate

the epitome of love and partnership
in sickness and in health
a missing part of a magical puzzle

deja vu, reconnections
synchronicity and understanding
spiritual connections

falling in love with flaws
unimaginable, a life without the other
comfort, confidence and intimate eye contact

communication without words
chemistry without sight
waking up with peace.

chasing silence

early morning hours filled with writing
fresh fallen snow glistening a carpet of white glitter
moments after a storm, a sky of gratitude
reflection within my thoughts and cultivated pauses
the stillness of solitude
beauty in nature's sounds
the peacefulness of my lover lying at my side
amidst the chaos of life
chasing silence

a redneck love story

shielding me from crowds
controversy
conflict
and his infidelity
    my redneck man
holding my hand for reassurance
sitting in the middle of the front seat
in the pick up truck
on the dirt backroads
    bonfires
      hotsprings
indulging my love of nature
    and solitude
protecting my secrets
yet keeping your own
the only remains of our redneck love story
    a photograph
a blanket partially covering you
laying on the cabin bed
broad, smooth shoulders
and unruly hair
the smell of pine and bonfire
envelops the afterglow of
    our last audacious twilight

life goes on

stop leaving out the parts of the story where you
screwed up
it doesn't matter who your past lovers were
what happened in your marriage or relationships
that you drank too much
or ate too much junk food with the kids
perhaps you wore your pajamas all day
or are still wearing yesterday's yoga pants
but these are only the trivial things
better to fail
        be defeated
                face adversity
                      be embarrassed
                              get discouraged
    ...life
            ...goes
                    ...on

wildfires

ignited by the dry lightning
of skin on skin sparks
in the illuminating glow
of the scintillating night

soul joy

language of possibility

community

imagination

vision

dream

laughter & happiness

wonder

change the world

together

enjoy the little things

soul joy

love regardless of colour

a conversation with my grandmother
about my unfruitful love life
always an inquirer into my current romantic
situation,
she asked me,
"What are you waiting for?"

"well, I haven't met anyone
 that I would want to
spend the rest of my life with,
especially not when I spend my time
between two provinces"

"have you ever met anyone
you wanted to spend the rest of your life with?"
Gigi asked candidly

"Yes. Remember? In Quebec."

"your grandfather was an idiot with his notions
always being a jackass to you kids
we didn't even go to your cousin's wedding
mind you
that marriage didn't last long
and she had a few more after it"
Gigi rambled

"Grandfather was an idiot,
but you both were the ones who
ranted about interracial marriage years ago
and not coming to my wedding
if I married a black man,
let alone a French speaking black man"
I countered
"I have dated nothing but depressed white men since"

"I am an old fool
You need to love regardless of color"
she declared in
our last meaningful conversation before her passing

on second chances

it takes a strong person to give
someone a second chance
to resolve regret
learn from mistakes

patience
wisdom
forgiveness
courage
grace

some of the most beautiful moments
won't happen the first time around
the universe changes
letting the real magic happen
on second chances

gypsy soul

I am grateful
for love
joy
and possibility

I am grateful
for encouragement
compassion
and non-judgement

I am grateful
to live with creativity
inspiration
and emerging artistic identity.

I am grateful
for being independent
unpredictable
and creating my own story

I am grateful
for having a free spirit
a messy life
and a gypsy soul

Acknowledgements

With gratitude to my editor, Deb Martens, for her wisdom, faith, friendship and editing skills.

To my son, my greatest gift, for his patience and never ending encouragement for every project.

I must thank my group of readers. Without these ladies encouraging me to "write more" or "tell me the story behind that poem," I may not have finished creating this book.

Appreciation to my writerly friends who encouraged me to explore poetic inquiry as a research method to capture my autoethnography of life and love with authenticity through poetry.

Indebtedness to lazy Sundays and the cabin on the river that brings silence, peace and creativity, sparking the words onto paper.

To the people who graced my life with moments of love and laughter. To the failed relationships that have inspired poetry and made me believe in never settling for bad coffee, having the courage to live and learn, and always chase of butterflies.

About the Author

A homeschool mom, researcher, writer and poet, E.D. Woodford currently spends time between BC, Saskatchewan and the Pacific Northwest writing poetry and contemplating what her PhD question may be. She is passionate about art, poetry, photography and organizing writing retreats and workshops as co-founder of Wildflower Writing Workshops.

Embracing her Sioux-Metis background, E.D. Woodford teaches post-secondary in Education, First Nation Studies, Anthropology and Sociology. She has a Baccalauréat en Éducation from the University of Alberta and a Masters of Arts from The SelfDesign Graduate Institute in Washington. In her current research, she is exploring poetic inquiry and its practice in storytelling and auto-ethnography as qualitative research. The recent outcome of this exploration of life and love with authenticity is this debut poetry collection: *Wild Heart. Gypsy Soul.*

Made in the USA
San Bernardino, CA
12 December 2017